Living In . . .

The Right House At the Right Time

*Residence Planning
For the Second Half of Life*

Judy Miller, Broker, M.Ed.

This publication is designed to provide accurate and authoritative information in regard to the subject matter covered. It is sold with the understanding that the author is not engaged in rendering legal, accounting, or other professional service. If legal advice or other expert assistance is required, the services of a competent professional person should be sought.

"It takes hands to build a house but only hearts can build a home."

~ Author Unknown

What People Are Saying About This Book

Judy has written a must read for homeowners and would-be homeowners who wish to treat their residence both as a financial asset and their own personal piece of the American Dream!

Jim Remley,
Author of *Sell Your Home in Any Market*
AMACOM/2008

Is it time to move, or time to stay put? Questions and the need for decisions assault you, often finding you unprepared and anxious. *Living in the Right House at the Right Time* provides a clear guide to walk you through this season of transition — option-by-option.

Lynn Leissler
Writer for *Southern Oregon Magazine*

This book is a thing of beauty and ingenuity. I have no doubts that if it had been published 10-20 years ago, we would have avoided the current housing crisis.

Guy Jenkins,
Tax Preparer

Judy brings a fresh, applicable perspective to residential planning for the second half of life. We plan for everything else but often manage our living environment by the seat of our pants, allowing life and its events to dictate important decisions.

This book brings our homes into the planning process, offering us better control of a very important component of our financial and emotional well-being. Judy approaches this subject with a rare depth of knowledge and tremendous compassion.

Cheryl C. Johnson, Wealth Advisor
SeaCrest Wealth Management

Table of Contents

PART I:
Residence Planning

Judy Miller
BROKER

Dear Friends,

I am a REALTOR® and CERTIFIED FINANCIAL PLANNER™ professional. When I transitioned from financial planning to real estate, I sensed a gap between these two disciplines, especially during the second half of your life. Your REALTOR® guides you through the purchase or sale of your property while your financial planner makes sure you have assets to buy it and income to maintain it. But you also have other important decisions and choices to make during this process.

The second half of life brings changes. We just don't know when or which ones. Who helps you maximize both your home's value as an investment and its functionality as your residence? Or determine the best time to sell and move? Our current planning process offers little or no guidance. This book introduces a new concept, *Residence Planning*, to provide that guidance.

Your home plays a vital role in providing you with a productive and fulfilling future. If you, or your adult children, (and hopefully all of you together,) are trying to come to grips with when to sell, buy another home, move to a residence community or stay where you are, this book will help you begin the process. I invite you to join me on the journey to find your answers.

Your Residence Planner,

Judy Miller, Broker, M.Ed.
 CERTIFIED FINANCIAL PLANNER™ (CFP®)
 Certified Residential Specialist® (CRS®)
 Certified Senior Advisor® (CSA®)
 Seniors Real Estate Specialist® (SRES®)

Part I:

Residence Planning

When it's time
to move forward

Residence Planning: Getting Started

Congratulations on beginning this book! You are taking the first step in making important and potentially life-changing decisions about your second half of life and where you will live. These decisions may not be easy, but they will put you on the path of personal control in the second half of your life.

The best place to start is by evaluating where you are today. *A Self-Assessment: Are you Living in the Right House?* is included at the end of this book. Candidly complete this questionnaire. The key is honesty. You need not share your answers with anyone, but you may want to ask a close friend or relative to review your answers and get their opinion. Then, after completing the questionnaire and discussion, return here to begin your exploration of Residence Planning.

Planning for Life's Later Years

As time passes, we age. Our homes age. In the second half of life, transitions seem to come more rapidly and require more decisions. Nothing is more foundational than our home.

Among the most complex decisions we make are deciding when and where to move. We may experience a decline in financial strength, the death of a spouse, or the absence of family or neighbors we were counting on. Our homes may not work as well for us as these changes occur. We don't know how long we will live or what our health needs will be. All these factors make it difficult to know how long to stay in our homes or when we should consider moving to one better suited to our needs or budget.

We gain a sense of control over our lives when we understand our housing choices and their compatibility with our physical abilities and financial resources. When we know our options, timeframes and required financial resources, we make choices that maximize the return on investment we want our homes to provide.

Your House and Your Home Aren't the Same Thing!

You buy and sell **houses**. You create and live in **homes**. Understanding the difference can help you recognize that a time will come when you can still love your home AND decide it is time to move.

A *house* is a building, a physical structure defined in specifics such as square footage, number of rooms and architectural style. It has a specific location and amenities such as a gourmet kitchen, shop or pool. You cannot convert this asset to cash quickly, but when you do sell, you expect to make money.

A *home* includes your house but it is also where you create an environment that's all your own, an expression of your personal identity, values, and traditions. It holds

4

your memories, your roots and all the "stuff" that's important to you.

Your home is three things:
- your largest financial asset
- your most complex emotional asset
- your most time-consuming physical plant asset

Your home requires money, time, energy and stamina. Since it is the house you expect to sell and the home you live in, your plan for the future must address all of these components.

Most of us want to live in our homes until the day we die. I have had more than one person tell me flat out, "I'm living here until they take me out in a pine box, and then I won't be here to care what happens!" That works for some, but not for most of us.

The second half of life is a lengthy period. It is an enormous mistake to conclude that because you can afford your home today, you are in good shape. Most people need guidance for maximizing their home's value and functionality over time. Planning is the key to your future.

Key Questions in Residence Planning

No single house is likely to match your life-style needs during your potentially lengthy retirement period. Three questions should be at the forefront for any decision you make regarding your home:

1. How will this decision affect my home's future salability?
2. How will it affect my future buyer pool?
3. How will it support my changing health and lifestyle needs?

Various professionals may help with residence planning but they are not likely to be able to give guidance on all the issues. People complete financial and retirement planning with their financial advisor and estate planning with their attorney. They work with their insurance specialist to protect their home against damage and destruction and provide money to pay off the mortgage if one of the owners dies.

However, we currently have no residence planning process to help us identify:

- where we would like to live
- where circumstances may require us to live and
- the factors that influence whether we sell our homes at opportune times and for the best price.

Failure to answer these questions carefully and consider potential consequences may be an expensive oversight in the end.

Residence Planning looks at who you are, where you live and what matters most to you. It is being honest about defining what you would like versus what you need and then using guidelines to help you know when it's time to sell and move.

Goal of Residence Planning

Assure quality living in a home that maximizes both your investment and its functionality over time.

Residence Planning helps you clarify your priorities and consider the impact of life, health and cognitive changes that may occur. Perhaps the greatest value of Residence Planning comes from thoughtfully and carefully addressing when and where you move. All too often, people make these decisions during a crisis when thinking is muddled and crucial decisions must be made quickly. No time is available for planning or considering future consequences.

During the planning process, you identify time frames or life events for selling and moving, and include your wishes for memorabilia, collectibles, and antiques. You share this information with your Stakeholder Team—your family and circle of professional advisors.

If you don't address these issues and don't make appropriate decisions for yourself, life may make them for you. You may find yourself in a situation you did not choose, don't like and deeply resent. In the final analysis, a person's indecision or refusal to address these issues often creates his or her unhappiness. You can prevent this by proactively making healthy choices for your home and location.

If you tackle the hard questions now, you can maintain your independence longer and maximize your home's value when you do sell. You will be in a position to move at a time and to a place that meets your needs and makes you feel comfortable. In addition, you may improve your access to health care providers and services so you can spend more time on activities you enjoy. You may feel safer and more secure. When you reduce the worry of becoming a burden to your family and friends, you remain in control and create an enjoyable and fulfilling life.

How Residence Planning Works: Meet Tom and Linda

Let me introduce Tom and Linda,[1] who wanted to explore their concerns about the future suitability of their home. They are in their mid-50s and adore the home they built: a 4,500 sq. ft., four-bedroom, three-floor home with a pool and gorgeous views of the valley.

They knew that climbing the stairs was becoming a problem, so they had already talked with an architect about converting their two-car garage off the kitchen into a 1,500 sq. ft. master bedroom/bath suite and adding a detached garage. They could afford the $250,000 projected cost, but thought it would be a good idea to get a REALTOR's® opinion. The concept of Residence Planning was new to them.

---

[1] Fictitious names. All scenarios are a composite of various clients with whom I have worked over time.

We started by talking about their dreams and potential physical limitations. Difficulties with climbing stairs would one day eliminate the entire upper floor where all the bedrooms are. The house also has a steep driveway and steps up to their front door. These were concerns as well.

We talked about who would be potential buyers for their home. Its current layout is particularly well suited to families with children and teenagers.

If they added a first-floor master suite, that would change the attractiveness to buyers. We talked about who would want to buy a home with two large master suites on different levels. A family that included a grandparent was a possibility. But having a grandparent on the upper level would be frustrating to both children and the grandparent. It would be equally disturbing to have a grandparent right off the kitchen and adjacent to the main traffic corridor in and out of the house. We could not readily identify potential buyers who would want two master suites in these locations.

The next question was whether a four-bedroom, 4,500 sq. ft. home or a five-bedroom 6,000 sq. ft. home would be more attractive to potential buyers. We all agreed the larger home would be more difficult to sell and that the proposed remodel would probably reduce their home's future value and buyer pool.

We considered costs for maintenance. If they remained in the home, they would have to hire out much of the work. They would have the cost and hassle of overseeing the workers and the turn-over among service providers. Long-term costs include replacements for the roof, heating system, air-conditioning system and several appliances. The exterior would also need repainting.

We agreed that they would likely see a significant increase in utility and other costs in the future. This would be especially painful if they were not using the upper floor. They would be paying for heating, air conditioning, property taxes and mortgage interest on unoccupied space.

Today's buyers are already beginning to prefer smaller homes to larger ones. If this trend continues as expected, the buyer pool for their home would shrink even further.

I asked Tom and Linda whether they were willing to accept a financial loss from the get-go. If their $250,000 remained in their investment accounts and grew at 5% a year, it would be worth $580,000 in 15 years. We all agreed that they probably would not recoup this investment in their home's future appreciation.

They had never thought of the impact of their proposed remodel on their future buyer pool and salability of their home, or the high probability that the remodel would decrease their personal financial worth. They both experienced grief, a reaction that is very normal with the loss of a life dream. A few months later, we had a follow-up discussion that considered additional components of their Residence Plan.

Readiness and Resource Planning

Readiness and resource planning develops strategies for accepting your increasing limitations without losing quality of living. It acknowledges the changing roles of your adult children in your life and identifies community support services to support your needs as your abilities change.

You consider many factors in readiness and resource planning:
- Affordability
- Appropriateness
- Community connection
- Accessibility
- Safety and security

For the best results, include your family and planning professionals in this process.

Affordability

Affordability is the basis for all residence planning. Your available cash and cash reserves have to support all expenses, mortgage payments, taxes and long-term maintenance costs for your property over a period of years.

Over time, costs increase because of inflation, the increasing age of your home and your decreasing physical abilities to maintain it yourself. When fixed incomes do not keep up with these increasing costs, you may find yourself drawing down income-generating assets or you may become financially dependent on your family.

In addition to inflation, other financial forces exert pressures as well. Uncertain income sources or fluctuating yields on investments can play havoc with expectations for retirement income. For example, bank CDs were paying 9.9% interest in 1990. That year, a new Ford Taurus sold for $9,990. If you owned a $100,000 CD, your 9.9% annual interest of $9,990 would purchase a new car. In 2012, a new Ford Taurus cost approximately $25,000.[2] Bank CDs were paying 0.5% or $500 in annual interest on a $100,000 CD. Your $500 in interest would cover only your first month's payment!

Sometimes people use a Reverse Mortgage to provide needed cash flow. With this loan, you are spending your home equity today, and you have to pay it back from your sale proceeds when you sell your house. Carefully assess whether your reduced sale proceeds will be adequate to support your later-in-life financial needs such as increasing health care costs. You need to fully understand this complex and expensive loan product and the circumstances in which it would be appropriate for you.

In addition to cash and home equity, financial assets also include items such as antiques, furniture, rugs, art, china, silver, crys-

---

[2] Kelly Blue Book information.

tal, collectibles, power tools, RV or a boat. These items carry both hard (actual cash value) and soft (sentimental, emotional and family-based) values that play into your financial plans for the future. Adult children may want these items for themselves or their children. Family members may have different agendas, and they may or may not support your decisions.

Some of these items are valuable but highly illiquid, meaning you cannot convert them to cash easily. Unless you plan to sell them, it is not wise to include them as a source of income for your future.

If you do want to convert valuable items to cash, plan for their disposition and sale so you receive maximum value. That may mean waiting several years to find the optimum time to sell. Have these items professionally appraised so that you make wise choices when selling. With a plan in place, you won't be forced into a snap decision during a family crisis, such as a death or serious illness.

Appropriateness

Appropriateness looks at how well your home "fits" you in terms of your personal comfort, physical stamina, and lifestyle requirements. It considers the physical layout to see if your present house meets both current and future lifestyle needs and whether your neighborhood is safe and secure. Your family's comfort level with where you live is also important.

Community Connection

Community connection addresses your ability to get to others and others' ability to get to you. Access to your social and support network prevents social isolation that leads to depression, mental withdrawal and other health-related problems over time. It allows emergency personnel, people servicing your home, and caregivers to get to you. You are also able to easily get to medical appointments, hospitals, your place of worship, shopping, etc.

Community connection also plans for when you are no longer able to drive. Most women outlive their ability to drive by ten years and men by seven years. You need to identify how you will maintain your connection to your community apart from your car and whether walking, cycling, and/or public transportation are viable alternatives.

Accessibility

Accessibility refers to how readily you can use features of your home. High shelves may be off limits because of poor balance. You may have difficulty reaching into under-bed storage bins, bottom shelves of cabinets or the dishwasher. Stairs may eliminate access to bedrooms or a laundry room.

If you have difficulty moving about your home, climbing stairs or getting in and out of the bathtub, you may require some home modifications. (Discussed in a later section.)

Safety and Security

Safety and security planning addresses whether you are protected and free to be yourself in your home. This may include having a security system, assistive technology or someone who phones regularly to check in. It also focuses on preventing falls throughout your home and yard. A second aspect looks at whether your neighborhood will continue to be safe and secure or whether its deterioration leaves you vulnerable. Neighbors you were counting on may have moved away.

Your Stakeholder Team

Your Stakeholder Team is your broad circle of family and professional advisors who assist with or need to be informed about your housing-related decisions. Though you usually make the final decisions, your adult children are generally involved, and may be the first to recognize the need for you to move or alter your living arrangement.

Your team of professional advisors can include many specialists. It should include a REALTOR® who is a Seniors Real Estate Specialist® (described in a later section). Your estate planning attorney creates your powers of attorney and healthcare directives that you may need when selling your home. Your CPA or tax planner evaluates potential estate and capital gains tax consequences from the sale. Others on your team may include your financial planner, insurance agent, geriatric care manager, doctors and other medical specialists, your pastor, priest or rabbi, and your guardian or conservator, if appointed.

Communicating your desires clearly to your Stakeholder Team is crucial so that in a crisis they may make decisions consistent with your wishes. The more you plan, explore options and work collaboratively, the better your residency decisions and transitions from one home to the next will be. Thorough planning enables you to remain in greater control of your life and the decisions affecting it.

What Are My Choices?

What you need and what you want in your home change as you move through life. You chose your home when you were younger and certain features were the best for you at that time. For example, those features that made your home great for raising children may now be expensive nuisances, such as the swimming pool you have to maintain, or the three-car garage that holds all your children's paraphernalia that they no longer use and you do not want!

The best solution may be to move to a smaller home much earlier in retirement. This reduces your monthly expenses for utilities, taxes, insurance and may eliminate or reduce mortgage debt. Lower expenses over a longer period of years may keep you afloat financially. You also save money by increasing the number of years you live independently and decreasing the time you live in a residence community.

If you relocate, you may reduce the amount of your driving. If you are closer to doctors, shopping and family, you save on gas, car maintenance and perhaps auto insurance. You may be able to eliminate a second car or drive a smaller one. Not only will this result in savings from lower costs, it may free up time for new interests, friends or activities you enjoy.

If you have a 10-25+ year life expectancy, chances are good that you will exercise several options for housing. It depends on whether you proactively plan to manage life, or whether you let life manage you. The silent thief to your home's future value comes when you do not factor in the impact of your lifestyle and health requirements on the future salability of your home.

Your choices for housing include:
- Staying put: maintaining the status quo
- Aging in place
- Midsizing
- Downsizing

- Moving to a residence community

During the second half of your life, you may exercise several of these options so that you are always living in the right house at the right time.

Staying Put: Maintaining the Status Quo

Sometimes staying put seems the best option. But make sure you objectively and seriously examine your reasons for doing so. You might find you are hiding behind one or more of the following reasons.

"I'm OK Right Now"

You are comfortable where you are and have no need to move. You have worked hard to get your home just the way you want it and you want to enjoy it. Go for it.

Be proactive as well, however. Be ready to move sooner while you have energy and stamina rather than later when your physical abilities begin to decrease. It is always better to move at a time you choose rather than when you must.

At some point, your comfort may become a mask that prevents you from acknowledging life changes you would rather avoid. You may become more vulnerable to falls, accidents and unexpected health events that your present home is not equipped to handle. Additional costs as your home ages may consume financial resources you need or want for other things.

"I Want Room for the Grandkids"

Our homes hold our families, and nothing is more special than a visit with children and grandchildren. The actual cost of these visits may surprise you and suggest that you rethink this priority.

Let's assume you have an extra bedroom, bath and living space that you only use for occasional guests. These three rooms total 450 sq. ft. The monthly expenses for your 2300 sq. ft. home total $2,600. This means you spend $1.13 per sq. ft. each month or $500 a month for this 450 sq. ft. space that you almost never use. That is $6,000 a year.

If your grandchildren come to see you for a week every other year, that visit costs you $12,000 or about $1,700 a day! This does not include food, entertainment or transportation. I can almost see your horror. You never write a check to pay this bill so you are completely unaware of this drain on your cash flow.

If you decide to live in your home for another fifteen years, this additional space will cost you $90,000 in after-tax dollars. In addition, you will have to clean and maintain this space. In all likelihood, it fills up with the superfluous "stuff" that you have to sort, organize and move when guests visit or you eventually move.

Based on the life expectancy of appliances and mechanical systems, in the next 15 years your home would require new heating/air conditioning, roof, hot water heater, dishwasher, refrigerator and exterior painting at a future cost of $32,000.

Your total expenditure will be:

Extra Space	$90,000
Maintenance	32,000
TOTAL	$122,000

If you are in the 25% tax bracket, your before-tax cost is $152,500. Is paying for unused space the highest and best use of your assets? Or would you rather spend this amount on college educations for your grandchildren or travel for yourselves?

"I'm Waiting for the Market to Come Back"

You may want to stay put so that your home bounces back in value after the recent downturn. But how long will that take? I recently talked with a couple whose home had dropped in value to $250,000 and they weren't planning to sell until they could get $375,000. If real estate appreciates at 4% a year, it will take 11 years to reach this price.

I asked them if they had the financial resources and physical energy required for maintenance over the period. They hadn't considered this and weren't sure.

In 11 years they would spend $95,700 for extra space and long-term replacement costs. They would only realize $29,300 or 23% of their desired $125,000 when they sell their home. Hidden numbers tell a compelling story.

Staying put and maintaining the status quo may be the most expensive option. For most people, this money slips through their fingers and they never realize what they are costing themselves in terms of future financial security.

Aging in Place

Aging in Place and its companion concept, *Aging with Choice,* expects that you can cope successfully amid declining abilities, either by yourself or with assistance from family or caregivers. This option enables you to remain in your home and live independently or with the assistance of family or other caregivers.

Support Services

You may require additional professional resources at some point. Homemaker services for non-medical needs include personal care, meal preparation, laundry, light housekeeping, shopping or respite care. In-home health care requires your physician's supervision and licensed health care professionals for medically prescribed assistance. You want an advisor or Geriatric Care Manager who is thoroughly familiar with covered Medicare services to review your eligibility.

If you have a Long Term Care Insurance policy, check to see whether it covers these services. Do not assume this. Ask your insurance agent to explain this coverage to you long before you need it. This coverage does not begin until your doctor confirms to your insurance company that you are unable to care for yourself according to your policy's provisions.

Home Modifications

When a health problem suddenly arises, features of your home that you took for granted can now cause major difficulties. These include thermostats that are accessible only when standing, outlets behind furniture that are unreachable, narrow hallways that require tight turns, slippery wood floors with throw rugs, towel bars that collapse when grabbed in an emergency, or toilets that are too low to use safely or comfortably. Unexpected life events force you to recognize the limitations they cause.

When you are faced with declining physical abilities, home modifications allow you to adapt your home so you have full use of it. You install products that blend well with your decor and are adaptable to change when the time comes. One important goal is to prevent falls.

Simple modifications can make life easier and safer without much cost. Quick and easy changes include increasing the wattage on lighting and adding a shower chair. You can also install other items such as lower thresholds, grab bars in bathrooms, lever doorknobs, stair handrails, and a security system.

Often people wait until they suffer an injury, and then they take a "Band-Aid" approach to cobble together adaptations to meet immediate needs. This approach often turns their home into a hospital. Usually there is not time to weigh decisions carefully. However, if moving is not an option in this situation, home modifications may be your only choice.

You may also think about a major remodel to make your home more accessible for your changing physical needs. If you are contemplating a remodel, talk to professionals who can help you consider the costs versus the gains and whether the remodel is consistent with the overall design of your home. Employing an architect to design your remodel is probably the best investment you can make to retain the basic character of your home and accommodate modifications you require.

Other professionals are also helpful when considering a major remodel. They can help you determine the effect of the remodel on future price and salability of your home. Consult a Certified Aging-in-Place Specialist® and a Seniors Real Estate Specialist® or a REALTOR® when you are considering relocating appliances, changing counter heights, enlarging showers, widening doorways and adding access ramps.

These professionals help you consider how your buyer views these changes. What is their impact on future salability and your buyer pool? Professionals know what does and doesn't sell in your market and can tell you whether you are increasing the appeal of your home as a buyer views it.

Remember that home value is always buyer-perceived. When you sell your home later, if your buyer sees a hospital instead of a dream home, your home may not be as desirable for their needs. Therefore, the value of your home decreases. If you have changed your home's character, you run the risk of losing the money you have invested and reducing your buyer pool when you do sell. Be aware, too, that remodels do not return 100 cents on the dollar when you sell.

Your financial strength is also important. How will you pay for the modifications or remodel? Can you afford an additional monthly payment if you take on additional debt? Will you have to curtail spending or sacrifice lifetime dreams? Perhaps you could liquidate assets. Review options with your financial advisor so you do not inadvertently create problems further down the road.

Trying to stay put may wind up being your most expensive alternative. From a financial standpoint, moving early in retirement may be your best option and midsizing may be your best answer.

Midsizing: A Strategy to Maximize Your Financial Strength

Midsizing is moving early in your retirement years to a home that continues your lifestyle today and anticipates changes in future years. Your current home may be the right size for you but may also have features that are not well-adapted to the future. A home better suited for your second half of life may free you from the financial and physical demands of an aging home and create time for travel or new interests.

You also reap financial rewards if you are able to live more years in your midsize home and decrease the number of years you live in a residence community. If this is a new(er) home, you have more years for your savings to grow before you have to replace aging appliances and mechanical systems. You are even stronger financially if you sell before you have to replace them.

Selling now may be your best long-term strategy. Younger buyers provide a built-in buyer pool for your current home. Now may be the optimum time to sell it for maximum financial gain.

Since we are on the leading edge of the Boomers entering the second half of life, the last of them will be arriving at retirement age when you are ready to sell the house you buy today. They will want your "midsize" home for the same reasons you did. This gives you a built-in buyer pool when you are ready to sell 15-30 years from now allowing you to reap maximum benefits from this home sale as well.

The decision to move from a home you love that is working well for you is one of the most complex and difficult ones you consider. How do you decide whether your current home is the best choice for your second half of life? Answering these questions may help you decide if midsizing is the answer.

- Do you have to climb steps to enter your home?
- Is your home two-story?
- Is your master bedroom on an upper floor?
- Is it easy to get groceries from the garage into your kitchen?
- How soon do you need to replace the roof, heating/air conditioning system, appliances or windows? Would it be better to sell your home now when you have a buyer pool wanting what your home has to offer?
- What health benefits could you realize? For example, would your knees benefit if you didn't climb stairs regularly?

The younger you are when you move, the easier it is. First, you have more energy, physical stamina and independence today than you will later. If you are married, you have someone to share the whole process with you. Many people feel rejuvenated when they are free of the stuff they no longer use or need. Midsizing may be your ticket to a golden future.

Downsizing to a Smaller Home

Downsizing is the process of selling your current home and moving to a smaller or less expensive one. Downsizing does not mean trading down your lifestyle, and it may actually enhance it. Even if you move later in life and have fewer years to reap the financial rewards, you still gain savings from a smaller home.

Answer the following questions to help you decide if downsizing is your best choice.

- Do you have rooms you no longer use or more space than you need?
- Can you easily afford to stay for 10-15-25 years? Do you want to afford this or would you prefer having additional money for travel or other interests?
- Are you hanging on to your large home for the few times your adult children and grandchildren might come for a visit?

Downsizing is a money-smart move. Financial wisdom suggests weighing the costs of staying in a home that may actually be too big for you. What would your lifestyle feel like if you had less to take care of and it cost you less to do so? A smaller and newer home might actually increase your financial strength over the long term, and protect your physical strength so that you are able to live independently for more years.

A smaller home reduces or eliminates your mortgage debt and frees up cash for other uses. You may be able to pay cash for your next home and eliminate your mortgage payment. If you are retired and not generating income, a monthly mortgage payment may become a greater burden over time. If you are withdrawing funds from retirement accounts to make these payments, you may trigger additional taxes. Unless the profit on the sale of your residence exceeds $250,000 for an individual or $500,000 for a couple, any gains from the sale of your home are usually tax-free.

Smaller homes generally have lower property taxes and lower expenses for utilities, yard care, home maintenance, and homeowner's insurance. When things get old and need replacing, you buy a smaller roof, less carpet, and maybe just one furnace instead of two. If you are moving to a different community or state, you may enjoy a lower overall cost of living, as well.

A smaller home is an excellent opportunity to strengthen your overall financial position for life's later years when you need it most. If you save $500 a month for the next ten years, and that money earns 3% it would grow to $70,000. If it earns 7%, it would grow to $86,500. It is never too late to start saving.

Today's real estate trends already point to Americans preferring smaller homes over larger ones. In the future, when you are ready to sell your smaller home, you have a strong Boomer buyer pool waiting which translates into financial gain when you sell. Beyond saving money and strengthening your financial position, downsizing could dramatically improve your health, safety and quality of life.

To help your decision-making, get an accurate picture of what you are spending on your current home each month. Complete the following chart so you can compare your current expenses with other options. Then, decide which is your best choice financially. If you live on a fixed income, be conservative in your estimates. A good rule of thumb is to have six months of living expenses saved in a designated account so you can handle unexpected house-related emergencies.

Expense	Current Home	Smaller Home	Residence Community
Mortgage or Rent	$	$	$
Property Taxes	$	$	*Included*
Homeowners' Insurance	$	$	*Included*
HOA Fees (if any)	$	$	*Included*
Electricity	$	$	*Included*
Gas	$	$	*Included*
Water/Sewer	$	$	*Included*
Waste Removal	$	$	*Included*
Housekeeping	$	$	*May be Included*
Maintenance or Repairs	$	$	*Included*
Yard Care	$	$	*Included*
Cable TV	$	$	*Not Included*
TOTAL	$	$	$

Medicaid planning is beyond the scope of this book. An advisor who is knowledgeable about Medicaid can help you determine the impact of selling your home on your future Medicaid eligibility. This may be your CPA, elder-law attorney or financial advisor.

Selling your home is a complex emotional decision that is complicated by the financial decisions you are making simultaneously. Especially if you have lived in your home for a long time, you grieve the loss when you move. Give yourself emotional space to acknowledge and process your feelings.

Some people have a Memory Celebration Party where you, family and friends reminisce. Tears and laughter are both healthy. If you are downsizing your personal items, you may set these out and invite your guests to take mementos as they leave. You gain pleasure knowing others are enjoying your treasures.

Moving to a Residence Community

Times have changed since we were children visiting grandparents in gray-walled nursing homes. Today, you have many options and combinations of living arrangements among residence communities. You can find the services you require along with the atmosphere and activities you enjoy. You pay monthly rent in addition to fees for other services you may require.

Adult Foster Homes

Adult Foster Homes offer personal and health care to individuals in private residences. They are a homelike alternative to nursing homes and offer various levels of assistance and care.

Assisted Living Facilities

Assisted Living Facilities provide private apartments and support services for people with mild physical or cognitive impairments. Personal and home care services may include meals, nutrition, housekeeping assistance and social activities. Home health care may also be available and may include medications management. Costs and required licensing of providers differ depending on the services they offer. These facilities often accept pets. Costs vary widely.

Continuing Care Retirement Communities

Continuing Care Retirement Communities (CCRCs) are made up of independent living residences, assisted living/residential care facilities and lifetime nursing care, if needed. They may also offer memory care options. They require residents to sign a contract, and pay an entrance fee in addition to other expenses. Review the contract carefully with your attorney before signing it.

Independent Living Communities

Independent Living Communities are for people who desire and are able to live independently but do not want to maintain a home. Services may include housekeeping, meals in a common dining room, social and recreational activities and exercise fitness centers.

Memory Care or Alzheimer's Care Units

Memory Care or *Alzheimer's Care Units* specialize in care for people with cognitive and memory impairment. These are secure buildings that alert staff if a resident has exited and provide a secured outdoor area where residents may enjoy some freedom.

Skilled Nursing Facilities

Skilled Nursing Facilities provide skilled services and nursing care for the chronically ill on a 24-hour basis. Nurses generally monitor and administer medical care prescribed by your doctor. They have doctors on staff, and may have physical and occupational therapists as well. They offer physical rehabilitation and recuperation after hospitalization for serious illness or surgery.

Information Resources

Fortunately, you have many resources for learning what your options are. Search the Internet for further information. The AARP website is excellent. Visit the communities in your area and talk with friends who live there. Your next "right" home is waiting for you.

Residential Inertia

Residential inertia is simply overstaying your welcome in your own home. If your home is larger than you need, it costs you more than necessary. You are probably not keeping up with routine cleaning and home maintenance because you no longer have the energy or physical capabilities this requires. Your pocketbook is shrinking unnecessarily.

As your physical or cognitive abilities decline, you become less able to remain independent, safe and secure in your home. When the decline is gradual, you may not recognize the extent of your losses or your inability to manage in ways that keep you safe.

People with residential inertia often become unequivocal about staying put. Change is frightening and the unknown unthinkable. They resist efforts from anyone who tries to talk to, reason with, or cajole them. They are not going to leave their homes – period.

Residential inertia is costly in terms of human relationships as well. Your family may be inept as caregivers or they may not have the time your increasing care requires. What happens when you are no longer able to drive and public transportation isn't an option? Neighbors you were counting on move away. Government cutbacks force a reduction in services you were counting on.

Often, an external event of some type forces resolution. I saw a home where the bottoms of the kitchen cabinets above the stove were badly burned because the owner forgot the pan of bacon on the stove. Or you fall, and no one finds you for a long time. Once residential inertia sets in, it is difficult to resolve, and both you and other family members may experience increasing tensions.

If you live in your home beyond its appropriateness for your needs, you may be at a point cognitively where you make poor decisions that cost you money, strain family and caregiver relationships, and force others to make decisions for you.

Oh No! The Unexpected Life Event Happens. . .

Stroke, heart attack, a fall and a broken hip. Your family swoops in. Doctors say, "You can't go home." You have done no planning or told anyone your preferences in this situation. Your family has no clue where you would like to live once you leave rehab and you are not in a position to be making these decisions now. They have no option but to find your next home and move you into it.

We are all vulnerable to these life forces. We cannot prevent the unexpected. But we can consider the "what-ifs" and decide what we would want in case one of these possibilities happens. When you have a Residence Plan that you have shared with your family and Stakeholder Team, you are in control of your life to the greatest degree possible in this situation. With no Plan, your family is clueless, and though they do their very best, you may be miserable and stuck with their choices. Depression sets in; you are inconsolable and may fight back, making both your life and theirs miserable.

Now your house sits empty with no one to take care of it. All too often, I have seen the house lose value and become a throwaway. With so much to think about, the family grabs a REALTOR® and says, "Sell it and get it off our hands." A desperation sale generally results in a lower price. No one has the time to think through the sale and work through the pre-sale process so that your house is in prime condition when it goes on the market. You are not there to help sort through your possessions, and prized collectibles or memorabilia do not go to the people or places you wanted.

When you move before life events force you to, you take control of your choices, save money, and enjoy the positive changes.

Part II:

Managing and Maintaining Your Home

When it's time to move forward

Home Ownership: Managing Your Financial, Emotional and Physical Energy Accounts

It takes more than money to manage a house. Your house requires money, energy and dedication to maintenance. These form the three accounts associated with home ownership:

- Financial
- Emotional, and
- Physical Energy

When these accounts are all balanced, you enjoy your home more. If they are out of balance, tension, worry and anxiety often increase.

Your desire for maintaining your home is likely to diminish as you grow older, and your willingness or enthusiasm for doing chores wanes. When you are unable to pay someone else to do chores you cannot or no longer want to do, resentment may build. Depression or stress may aggravate physical conditions when you attempt to do things beyond your current capabilities. You experience both financial and emotional costs.

These three aspects of your home cannot be separated. They become increasingly important when the second half of life requires unfamiliar and sometimes unexpected adjustments. When you understand how they interrelate, you can make better decisions about how you invest your time, money and stamina in your home.

Managing "Account Decisions:" Meet Jan and Ron

Jan and Ron own a large house that has become overstuffed with antique furniture that they are ready to sell or give to their adult children. Jan and Ron are in their mid-70s, in good health and believe they can live independently for at least ten years barring unforeseen health changes. They want to dispose of a large portion of the furniture so they can move to a newer and smaller home that suits their lifestyle and financial resources. A professional appraiser valued the furniture at $8,000.

Their adult children do not support their parents' decision to move or sell the antiques. They grumble because their parents will no longer have room for the extended family to come home for visits. They will miss their childhood haunts, and they are sad that the cousins will miss building special bonds.

Jan and Ron consider two possible solutions and the impacts on their financial, emotional and physical energy accounts.

Scenario A: Don't Sell and Don't Move

In this possible solution, Jan and Ron placate their adult children and do not sell the antiques or the house. Since the house is overcrowded, though, they rent a storage unit for ten years for $6,000 in hopes their adult children or grandchildren will have a place for their antiques someday.

Effect on "Account Balances"

Jan and Ron foot the bill (financial) with no appreciation from their children (emotional). They think about all the things they could do with $14,000 ($8,000 from the sale of the furniture plus $6,000 that they wouldn't spend on storage) and resent the whole situation (all three accounts). They worry about the effect of the storage environment on the antiques (emotional) and wonder whether the furniture is losing value as a result (financial).

In addition, they begin to experience problems with the house being less suited to their aging health (emotional and physical energy).

Scenario B: Sell and Move

In this possible solution, Jan and Ron find ways to satisfy their needs while considering what is important to their family, too. To accomplish all these goals, they develop a three-step plan.

Step One: Sell the Antiques

First, Jan and Ron offer their children the opportunity to have the antiques now as part of their inheritance, but each declines. They sell the antiques to younger friends who want the furniture in their new home. They invest the $8,000 in an account earning 5%.

Effect on "Account Balances"

Jan and Ron have several positive effects of this action.

- In ten years, their investment account grows to $13,200 (financial).
- They have liquidity with investments versus illiquidity with antiques (financial).
- They sell the antiques at an appropriate time and for an appropriate price (financial and emotional).
- They avoid a possible distress or forced sale due to an unexpected emergency (all three accounts).

- Jan and Ron know the antiques are in a place they chose and where they will enjoy seeing them in the future (emotional).

Step Two: Move to a New House

Jan and Ron purchase a newer, smaller, single-level home and save $800 in monthly expenses.

Effect on "Account Balances"

All three account balances benefit from this step.
- Jan and Ron are able to remain independent in their new home for more years so they feel in greater control of their lives (emotional).
- Their day-to-day lifestyle in their new home is well suited to their changing physical needs (emotional and physical energy).
- Their home's value appreciates over time (financial).

- They invest the $800 each month and (with interest and appreciation) their investment account grows by $125,000 over ten years (financial.)
- They are better prepared for later-in-life expenses or travel dreams (financial and emotional).
- With a new home, they won't have to replace mechanical systems, so they preserve financial assets (financial).
- Their adult children have fewer obligations in caring for their parents as they grow older because their home requires less maintenance and is well suited for their needs (all three accounts).
- They have a large baby-boomer buyer pool when they are ready to sell (financial and emotional).

Step Three: Maintain Family Connections

Jan and Ron agree with their adult children that they want their entire family to continue getting together, so they allocate $300 a month to save for a family reunion at a family-friendly location every other year.

Effect on "Account Balances"

Everyone enjoys the family vacations and the huge legacy of memories they create (emotional). Several of the locations are on Jan's and Ron's bucket list (emotional).

Selling family antiques, a seemingly small decision, can have far-reaching consequences in all three accounts. What might have been a lemon — the sale of the antiques — can become lemonade with a host of positive outcomes for the entire family.

Home Maintenance

The condition of your home is crucial if you want to sell it for top dollar. You need the physical energy to maintain it yourself or the financial resources to have someone else do it for you. You also need the stick-to-itiveness to make certain it gets done either way. Your return on investment from proper maintenance cannot be emphasized strongly enough.

When You Can No Longer Maintain Your Home, It's Time to Move

When your answer to any of the following questions becomes an outright "no," it is time to move. Your safety, quality of life and financial strength improve when you do!

1. Are you capable of maintaining your home now and for as long as you live in it?
2. Do you want to invest your time, energy and financial resources to maintain it?
3. Can you afford to pay someone else to maintain it for you when you are no longer able or willing to perform these chores?

People who attempt maintenance tasks that they are physically unable to do safely often experience falls or other accidents that result in life-changing consequences. Tackling some chores may be a "penny-wise and pound-foolish" choice.

One of my clients was standing on a wobbling ladder cleaning gutters when she realized a fall in any direction might result in a broken neck. She instantly got off the ladder and has had her yard maintenance person clean her gutters ever since. She told me, "I can't manage a taller ladder and don't have a place to store it. My health is excellent and I have waited all my life for retirement and time to travel. No gutter is worth giving up these dreams."

Home Maintenance Checklist

Well-maintained homes sell more quickly and for a higher sales price. Maintenance includes **all** of the items in the following list, and this list is by no means complete.

Outdoor Chores

- Mowing, edging, sweeping, blowing yard debris, pruning, fertilizing, weeding
- Keeping the roof clear of leaves and debris, treating for moss
- Pruning back trees so they don't rub against roof (shortens roof life!)
- Straightening and cleaning out the garage

Inside Chores

- Doing laundry, preparing meals
- Shopping for groceries and putting food away
- Cleaning bathrooms, dusting, mopping, vacuuming, changing beds
- Wiping down kitchen appliances and cabinets
- Taking care of plumbing leaks and electrical problems
- Changing light bulbs

Seasonal Chores

- Cleaning gutters and downspouts
- Washing windows
- Spraying for insects
- Cleaning or replacing furnace filters and refrigerator coils
- Checking for drips or more extensive water damage
- Inspecting, cleaning and repairing the chimney flue/fireplace
- Replacing batteries in smoke and carbon monoxide detectors
- Checking the roof flashing for wind and rain damage (*Flashing* is the metal pieces used to seal the areas between the roof and chimney.)
- Testing the performance of circuit breakers by flipping them off and back on (A circuit breaker that repeatedly trips could indicate a short in the wiring inside your walls.)

Periodic Chores

- Having carpets professionally cleaned

- Checking and replacing caulking and weather stripping around windows and doors
- Repairing or replacing broken screens
- Draining the hot water heater to flush sediment
- Checking and cleaning dryer vents and range hood filters
- Checking washer hoses and dryer vents

Longer-Term Maintenance

- Painting – interior and exterior
- Recoating, repairing or replacing driveway and walkway surfaces

I once worked with buyers where the husband walked into a home, found the furnace air filter, and if it was dirty, he walked out of the home. He was adamant: "If the sellers can't keep a furnace filter clean, what else are they ignoring?" The sellers lost a sales opportunity because of a dirty $15 furnace filter!

Life Expectancy of Appliances and Mechanical Systems

The following chart provides a guide for the number of years you can reasonably expect appliances and mechanical systems to last. When you know their useful life, you can be financially prepared to replace them when they fail.

- Air conditioner, central: 11
- Compactor: 6
- Dishwasher: 10
- Dryer, electric or gas: 12
- Exterior house paint: 5-10
- Furnace, gas: 15
- Furnace, electric: 15-50
- Freezer: 11
- Garbage disposal: 9
- Heat pump: 12
- Microwave oven: 9
- Range, electric: 16
- Range, gas: 17
- Range/oven hood: 11
- Refrigerator: 12
- Roof: 15-30
- Washer: 11
- Water heater, electric: 13
- Water heater, gas: 11
- Wood deck staining: 4-7

Let's assume that you want to live in your home for at least 15 more years. Based on the previous chart, let's look at the expenses you can reasonably expect for your home over that time period. This example assumes costs increase 3% annually.

Item	Years to Replace-ment	Cost Today	Future Cost
Heating/air conditioning	7	$6,500	$8,000
Dishwasher	9	$400	$525
Exterior paint	2	$4,000	$4,250
Exterior paint (required again)	12	$4,000	$5,700
Refrigerator	5	$1,300	$1,500
Roof	11	$8,500	$11,750
Hot water heater	8	$350	$450
Total			**$32,175**

Since all these major expenses come up within 12 years, you need to save $2,700 per year or have assets you can sell for future maintenance and replacement costs.

Another way to pay for home maintenance is borrowing from a Home Equity Line of Credit. This means an additional monthly payment and may require a reduction in monthly spending for the fun things you enjoy. You need to consider whether your housing costs will become a financial burden for you or your family in the future.

If You Fail to Maintain Your Home

What are the consequences of failing to maintain your home, especially over the long-term? Let's assume that your roof has exhausted its useful life when you're ready to sell. Your best option is to replace it before listing your home for sale. A buyer folds the cost into the loan and won't have to replace the roof for 30 years. This creates a win-win for both the buyer and seller.

Your next option is to lower your offering price by the cost of a new roof, but this poses problems. Your buyer will need funds to replace the roof soon after purchase, and this may eliminate some otherwise interested and qualified buyers. If the lender requires repair or replacement of the roof as a condition of your buyer's loan, you have to pay for the new roof before the sale closes or terminate the transaction.

Homes with deferred maintenance sell for less. In addition, your neighbors do not appreciate having your home in decline because this may lower the value of their homes. As the saying goes, you can pay now . . . or you will pay later. It is a fact: well-maintained homes that have no deferred maintenance sell for a higher price and in a shorter time than homes with maintenance issues.

Part III:

Selling and Moving

When it's time
to move forward

*Houses don't sell for
what they are worth. . .*

*Houses are worth
what they sell for.*

*Value is buyer-perceived.
Your home is worth what
a qualified buyer will pay
you for it.*

When is the Right Time to Move?

Many people struggle with the question of when to move. No one answer is right for everyone. Generally, the best time is when moving makes financial sense and it provides you with personal gains. These include lifetime dreams like being closer to family and grandchildren, and freeing up time for new interests, travel and friendships.

You get the best result when you move on your own terms and in your own timeframe. You **can** do it, and there are both ways and people available to help you accomplish all the steps in this transition.

Your family may recognize your need to move before you do. Generally, your children are your strongest advocates and only want what is best for you. They may be living in fear of the next phone call. Their concern is for your safety and what might be forced upon both you and them.

Rather than waiting until your physical condition forces it, move when you have maximum stamina and physical capabilities for bending, reaching high shelves, and dealing with heavy boxes. Your physical capability greatly enhances how well the move proceeds.

Procrastination and the fear of change are also obstacles to recognize and overcome. Procrastination plagues most of us, at least to some extent. You can always find reasons why staying where you are makes so much sense. This false evidence may gloss over gradual declines in your physical and cognitive abilities, eroding financial reserves, and declining ability to maintain your home.

Most people approach this transition with some fear and trepidation. It is physically, spiritually, and emotionally exhausting. Your head is telling you to do something while your heart may be screaming, "NO!" Your REALTOR® or Seniors Real Estate Specialist® gently helps you move forward and gives you space to process everything that is going on in your life.

Most people fear being caught with no place to go if their home sells before they have found the place where they want to move. The best solution may be to move to your new location first and then put your home on the market. This benefits both your REALTOR® and you. You can take the furnishings and personal belongings you want and go back to your home to exchange them if you find you want different items in your new home. Your REALTOR® can prepare your home for showings and know that it is always ready.

Find the Right Professionals

The most important decision in selling your home is selecting people you are confident can guide you through the decisions in your real estate transaction. You want professionals with insight and experience with later-in-life moves and a broad network of professionals and service providers to recommend when you need expertise in different areas.

A real estate agent and a REALTOR® are different. Both are licensed by your state to sell real estate. REALTORs® belong to the local, state and National Association of REALTORS® or NAR® . They have pledged to uphold the Code of Ethics and are subject to review and discipline for unethical business practices that violate this Code. In addition, REALTORS® may earn NAR® sponsored designations in specialized areas of real estate upon completion of additional education requirements. Two designations may help you find the right person: A Seniors Real Estate Specialist® and a Certified Senior Advisor®.

Seniors Real Estate Specialist®

A Seniors Real Estate Specialist® is a REALTOR® who is trained and uniquely equipped to guide you and your adult children through the complex issues and maze of decisions you are making. They have a passion for assisting you through this significant life transition.

Your SRES® listens deeply, gets to know you and your family, and is sensitive to the concerns you have about the move ahead. Though you usually make the final decisions, your adult children often help you think them through. Together you develop a plan for preparing your home to go on the market. Your SRES® helps you determine whether to repair or sell "as-is," re-carpet, re-paint, remove wallpaper etc. They recommend and schedule service providers and home repair specialists as needed.

Financial and legal considerations may come into play. For example, the sale of your home may generate capital gains on which you may owe taxes. If you have a reverse mortgage on your property, you must repay it when you sell. Some government benefits programs are means-tested: that is, individuals qualify based on their levels of income and assets. Many programs do not count your home as part of those assets. When you convert it to cash, this transaction could affect your qualification for benefits. These are examples of the issues you need to discuss with qualified professionals. Your SRES® is there to help if you become overwhelmed by these issues.

Finally, they have a specially designed process to help you sell or buy your home, and they tailor it to you. They explain their steps in detail, give you estimated time frames for completing each one and answer your questions until you feel comfortable. They are with you from start to finish.

Certified Senior Advisor®

Certified Senior Advisors® or CSAs® are trained in the interdisciplinary areas of finance, health and social issues as they pertain to second-half-of-life issues. Typically, CSAs® already have expertise in a professional discipline such as home care, real estate or financial planning, and have chosen to supplement that existing professional knowledge with the CSA® education. They know community resources to assist you in your next home and with the moving process. Their goal is to help you build toward a future where you can anticipate what your needs will be and plan to meet them.

An individual who holds both the Seniors Real Estate Specialist® and Certified Senior Advisor® designations understands life's broad picture in the second half of life. With their specialized expertise, they help you decide whether and when to move so that you maximize the value of your home and match your new one with your physical needs and financial resources.

Setting a Timeline

The first step in selling your home is setting a timeline. You might find it easier if you start with your ending date — when you want to move in to your new home or residence community. Your SRES® can estimate how long it is likely to take to market your home and close the sale transaction.

Another question is how much time you need to get your home ready to go on the market. What do you need to accomplish, what are you physically capable of managing, and what people are available to help? Part of this process is something that many people dread the most: downsizing your possessions.

The Allen Family's Proactive Plan

The Allen family worked together in preparing and selling the parents' home. The parents, Tim and Sheila, had already moved to a residence community and brought all the furniture, personal belongings and mementos they wanted. They had lived in their previous home for 38 years and, even after moving to their new place, most rooms in their old home still had wall-to-wall waist-high piles to go through. They were physically unable to do all the downsizing work. Although their three adult children lived out of the area, all wanted to come and help.

During a visit, their son, Bob, came with Tim and Sheila for a family consultation with me. The three of them set a schedule for completing the downsizing and the date for listing Tim and Sheila's home on the market. They agreed to sort and dispose of their important papers and have them professionally shredded to protect against identity theft. Bending over a shredding machine posed a potential health threat for both of them.

Then, the three adult children came for a five-day visit to clear out the house. They had a dumpster delivered to their parents' driveway. They divided the rooms in the house and each cleared out what they knew they could toss, and organized the remainder in piles for family, church rummage sale, Goodwill donations and throwaway. After this, they switched rooms and further reduced the piles.

As they worked, they shared family stories, memories, tears, laughter, frustrations and hugs. The three of them had not been together for a long time and they actually savored this special time. They were all very relieved that their parents had finally moved and loved their new apartment. But, most of all, they were glad both their parents were alive to answer questions about where things came from, how parts and pieces went together and where they wanted things to go. The children were thankful they would not have to do this by themselves following a funeral.

Finally, when all the sorting and initial tossing was complete, Tim and Sheila came to the house. They sat in the living room while the children brought items to them for final decisions. On the last day of their visit, they sent boxes to friends and relatives, took items to the church and Goodwill, and had the fully loaded dumpster hauled away.

Since they had lived in their home for so many years, Tim and Sheila followed my recommendation to have a Pre-Sale Full House Inspection before their home went on the market. We reviewed the report together, and I oversaw the required repairs. One involved decommissioning a 35-year-old oil tank. The purpose of taking care of these repairs is to increase potential buyers' confidence in the condition of their home. They would be able to see the report, receipts for all completed work and the Decommissioning Certificate for the oil tank. In addition, Tim and Sheila had the entire house professionally cleaned and the interior repainted so it looked fresh, bright and inviting.

The sales process went very smoothly. When their home went on the market (ten days ahead of their schedule!), it was turnkey ready for new owners. Nine days after we listed it for sale, Tim and Sheila accepted an offer.

One day I stopped by their apartment to get some paperwork signed and Tim, who had fiercely opposed the move initially, commented, "You know, Judy, we didn't live in all that space at the house. It mostly just got in the way. We have the same amount of living space here and this is so much better. Grocery shopping was a real hassle and lugging those bags in the house was really hard on my knees." It turns out he had met two Navy veterans who also served in World War II and the three of them thoroughly enjoyed getting together.

Downsizing Accumulated Possessions

We derive meaning and purpose from our possessions. They give us a sense of identity or status. Our closets full of clothes are how we create our sense of "self" and present ourselves to the world. Antiques may be links to our past that help us feel grounded today, and represent the legacy we want to leave for tomorrow. Sports team trophies are a source of pride and memories. Often, that's why we buy larger homes or rent storage units.

The problem for many of us is that we don't regulate our consumption of "stuff." We don't get rid of what we have before we add more. This becomes a problem because clutter actually claims energy, even if you just sit and look at it.

When clutter becomes excessive, your home may actually become more dangerous. Clutter often increases the risk of falling, and the consequences of falls become more significant as we grow older.

"Stuff" gets dusty and is time-consuming to clean. Not cleaning it can actually create health problems. The air quality in our homes might not be as healthy for us because of the excess dust and dirt.

If a move is coming in the next couple of years, methodically sort and get rid of unneeded papers and possessions. Do it now so that your available energy and stamina matches the task without overtaxing you physically. You reduce your stress levels considerably by de-cluttering.

For most of us, downsizing is a daunting proposition. This process is not easy or quick, but not downsizing may be keeping you prisoner in a home that no longer suits you. Give yourself time. When you get past your angst, you find the process manageable. You can gain a new lease on life by getting it done.

Despair and grief are part of the downsizing chaos. Remember that grief is a process, not a one-time event. Remind yourself that you are moving to a better future. Expect to feel overwhelmed from time to time. You can deal with it and still move forward. Drive down memory lane gently. Love something, cry over it and then give it away anyway. Tears and laughter will flow together.

Meet Your Downsizing Goals:
Keep the X's Moving

Comedian Jerry Seinfeld faithfully followed his habit of "Keep the X's Moving" so he remained sharp and fresh in his humor. He got a big wall calendar and hung it on a prominent wall. Every day he had to write one new joke, and when he completed it, he put a red X on his calendar. The moving chain of X's was a huge motivator for him. It can be for you, too.

Here is how you can set downsizing goals. If you already have an idea of the size home you wish to move to, base your downsizing strategy on the difference in space between the two homes. First, compare the size of your present home (number of square feet) with the size of your next home. For example, if your current home is 2,500 sq. ft. and you plan to move to a home that is 1,700 sq. ft., you lose 800 sq. ft. Then, divide the square footage you lose by the total square footage of your current home to determine the fraction of space you lose. In this example, 800 ÷ 2,500 = .32 or 32%. You need to reduce the possessions you move to your new home by about one-third.

This calculation becomes your "Downsizing Rule of Thumb" for your daily, monthly, or even longer term goals. Mark your calendar with an X each time you make progress toward your reduction goal.

Set small enough personal goals that you can meet them easily. Daily goals might be getting rid of one pile, or organizing and reducing one drawer. A monthly goal could be completing one entire room. A quarterly goal could be clearing a stuffed area such as the garage, attic or storage shed. Maybe you say "No watching football this fall until the garage is completely cleared!"

When you keep your X's moving, you make steady progress in reaching your downsizing goals. Success breeds more success. Celebrate along the way.

One Couple's Devotion

Recently, I worked with Diane and Jack, a couple who were ready for a smaller home with less yard care. While they were out for a drive one day, they saw their dream home.

Diane and Jack knew that downsizing would be difficult but they also shared this common goal. They knew that someday one of them would be left alone and downsizing then would be even harder. Doing this together would make it easier to work through all their accumulations, a chore they were dreading. I explained, "By the inch, it's a cinch. By the yard, it's hard!" They followed my suggestions and got the job done faster than they expected.

Now they are celebrating in their new and smaller home. They chose room colors and painted together. Jack enjoyed building shelves, adding a stained glass window and setting up a simpler shop for his tools now that he has gotten rid of all the ones he never used. After 53 years of mowing grass, he declared, "Enough is enough!" and left his lawn mower behind.

Diane had never had a walk-in pantry and she couldn't believe her smaller kitchen is actually more functional and enjoyable than the larger one she left behind. She loved making the window treatments with matching placemats and chair cushions for the dining area.

They deeply value the peace they share from knowing that the surviving spouse will have the home they created together without the dread and fear of having to move all alone. In the meantime, they are enjoying life enormously. The new deck is almost ready for their grill and the new recipes they've been collecting for it.

Diane and Jack were able to pay cash for their new home. With lower monthly expenses and no mortgage payment, they are more confident about their financial future and money for the traveling they've dreamed about.

Downsizing Defined!

I felt light-hearted as I was preparing to teach a class on Downsizing so I created the following acrostic that uses the first letter for DOWNSIZE. Enjoy!

Diligent **D**ecisions **D**emand **D**edication. Downsizing makes your home feel more spacious to a buyer so it sells more quickly.

Determine a workable plan and timeline for accomplishing it. Dedicate time regularly for your downsizing tasks. Divide items into categories: Keep, Family, Friends, Sell, Donate, and Throw Away. Donate, donate, and donate some more. Drive a load to Goodwill or Salvation Army at least once a week (or ask if they pick up). Discard unwanted items in a dumpster.

Own your **O**utcome.
Organize a timeline for completing your downsizing. Obtain references and get price quotes in writing for the service providers you plan to use.

Work at it and **W**hip this.
Who gets it? Where does it go? When does it leave your house? Work smart.

No **N**onsense.
No one expects you to do it all so ask for help. Never skip a target date on your timeline. Name the end-date for your downsizing – when you celebrate!

Stick-to-itiveness **S**purs **S**uccess.

Stop warehousing your kids' stuff. Stuff their items in boxes for them to take, and if they don't, then throw or give them away. Sell or auction items of value. Set a deadline or final date for your family and friends to get items they want. Stress that after this date, you will donate or discard their items. Stop and smell the roses, but be prepared to move along.

Initiate with **I**magination.

Inventory your physical limitations such as balance, high blood pressure, and ability to stand and lift heavy boxes. Identify what is hard for you and how you keep motivated. Increase the X's on your calendar!

Zest, **Z**eal and **Z**igzag

Zero-tolerance for not getting the job done is the key. Zigzag with the ups and downs (expect this, it's normal). Zones for sorting are helpful. Zoom in on memorabilia for each of your children: take pictures of their trophies, athletic letters and badge sashes.

Zealously create a photo book online as a Christmas or birthday gift; write your memories of these events and the book will be a real treasure.

Execute and Energize

Eliminate clutter and your home feels more spacious and is easier to sell. Energize yourself and have your own memory celebrations. Engage professionals like an appraiser, auctioneer, estate liquidator, and senior move manager. Expose and expel procrastination. Experience ecstasy when you're finished because you deserve it. Exude confidence; it's contagious.

Pre-Sale Preparation

Before you put your home on the market, take the following steps to get it ready.

Spic 'N Span Clean

Buyers notice cleanliness – the way your home looks and feels to them. This is both tangible and intangible. As we get older, we may not see stains, finger prints and dingy woodwork as clearly as we once did.

A sparkling clean home is your most important priority. This requires an in-depth cleaning like the spring cleaning your mother used to do:

- curtains down, washed, and rehung
- draperies thoroughly vacuumed or professionally dry cleaned
- windows washed inside and out so they are crystal clear with no streaks or spots
- walls washed to remove all spots
- woodwork washed
- closets sorted and straightened
- furniture moved and vacuumed
- and the list goes on.

Your best bet may be to spend the money for professional cleaning, especially if you are not physically able to manage this strenuous and demanding challenge. Now is also a good time to pack collectibles and books in preparation for your move. Your home looks more appealing when rooms have less in them.

If there are deferred maintenance issues, such as holes in walls or doors, cracks in vinyl floors, or a roof at the end of its useful life, you have some major decisions to make. If you want top-dollar for your home, you need to spend money to correct these problems. Or, you need to reduce your asking price if you plan to sell your home with these "as-is" conditions.

Curb Appeal

Your buyer forms their first impression when they pull up and park at the curb. You want the front of your home and your yard to show well. Consider hiring a lawn service to mow, trim and clean up the yard and prune overgrown shrubs and trees that conceal the home or obstruct impressive views. Have all your beds edged and add fresh bark mulch. Hire a handyman for basic repairs like patching cracks in sheet rock or fixing a sagging gutter.

Pre-Sale Full House Inspection

If you have lived in your home a long time, your REALTOR® may suggest you pay for a Pre-Sale Full House Inspection. This identifies needed repairs that you may not be able to see. Complete these repairs before your home goes on the market to demonstrate your commitment to your buyer to maintain your home. Also, you may close your transaction faster by avoiding lender-required repairs.

Buyers "fall in love" with your home as they are deciding to make an offer to purchase it. Sellers need to preserve this love affair by preventing hidden repair needs that could turn off the buyer. I once worked with buyers where the husband was wild about a house and made a very generous offer. When the Full House Inspection report named significant problems, I watched his wild enthusiasm sour, and he seriously considered terminating the sales contract. Fortunately, an additional inspection put his fears to rest and the sellers readily agreed to pay for the requested repairs.

If the sellers had completed a Pre-Sale Inspection and addressed these problems before their home went on the market, the buyers would have known about the problems and the repairs that were already completed. This would have demonstrated the sellers' commitment to maintenance and avoided the possibility of losing a sale.

Starting the Sales Process

You may have bought and sold homes before, perhaps several times in your lifetime. However, this time may be more complicated due to the number of issues to address, decisions to make and people to consult. The selling and buying process has changed significantly in just the past few years, in large part because of the Internet's impact on the way people get information about today's real estate market.

Selling your home is a partnership between your REALTOR® and you. As the seller, you are in complete control of setting the price and preparing your home for presentation to buyers. Your REALTOR® is responsible for promoting it to attract every ready, willing and qualified buyer to view it. He or she provides guidance in all these decisions.

Pricing

Contrary to popular belief when you are selling your home, its value is determined by one thing only: what a qualified buyer is willing to pay for it. A home without a buyer has no value in the marketplace.

Your initial offering price must be compelling so that it attracts agents to show your property and buyers to view it and make offers. Your REALTOR® [3] analyzes your property and will show you Comparative Market Reports about current

---

[3] The term REALTOR® includes an SRES® also.

market conditions and recently sold properties similar to yours. He or she recommends an offering price and discusses the factors that support it, but you, the seller, decide on the offering price.

Your home is competing for a limited number of buyers, and the first 21 days your home is on the market are critical. This is when interested buyers are excited to see if your home is what they want. You have the greatest opportunity to sell during this time. You should have immediate showings followed by an offer. If buyers are not coming to see your home after the first 8-10 days on the market, consider lowering your offering price so you make the best use of this critical first 21-day period.

Statistics from the National Association of REALTORS® show that 20-35% of homes sell in the first 30 days, a smaller number sell in each of the next five months, and 30-75% do not sell in the first six months. Research confirms that price is the number one reason a property does not sell. Your offering price needs to attract buyers immediately. Generally, the longer your home sits on the market, the lower your sales price is when your home finally does sell. Overpricing your home initially can wind up costing rather than making you money.

You need to recognize that no amount of marketing convinces a buyer to purchase an overpriced home. Value is buyer-perceived. Buyers are under no obligation to buy any particular home so they have no motivation to buy one that is overpriced. If buyers believe your home is comparable to your neighbor's, they will choose your neighbor's less expensive home over yours. Overpricing your home actually helps your neighbor sell theirs.

If your home is vacant while it is on the market, that can affect your pricing. The longer your house is unsold, the higher your carrying costs for property taxes, utilities, insurance and maintenance. You may actually make more money by selling quickly at a lower price and avoiding long-term carrying costs.

Presentation

Homes in top condition are likely to attract the most buyers and receive the highest offers. Because of the competition in our marketplace, your home is in "a price war and a beauty contest." It needs to be "Market Ready" on day one. You only have one chance to make a good first impression. How a potential buyer experiences your home makes all the difference.

Your home has a broader appeal to buyers when it does not indicate a particular age or stage in life. A prospective buyer may not see your home as appropriate if medicine bottles, a wheelchair or a raised toilet seat are in view. If you have already moved to your new home, your REALTOR® can pre-pare the home you are selling so it is "show-ready" whenever an agent wants to show it to a prospective buyer.

To help prepare your home, your REAL-TOR® walks through it with you and discusses changes that make it more appealing to buyers. The REALTOR® works with you to identify personal items to remove and pack in preparation for your upcoming move. The goal is to make your home look spacious.

In addition, you discuss any needed repairs and decorating changes, such as removing family pictures or repainting rooms. A room painted in a very strong or unusual color is likely to be more appealing if it is repainted in a more neutral color.

These changes make your home more attractive to buyers. This sounds so simple, but in reality, sellers find it very hard to view their home through a potential buyer's eyes. This is another example of how a REALTOR® presents expertise in sales.

Staging, a new process emerging today, addresses how to make your home more visually attractive to buyers. Your REALTOR®

may suggest that you employ a Stager or, if he or she has the expertise, the REALTOR® may direct you through the process. The goal is to reduce the contents of rooms and neutralize them so they appeal to a broad cross-section of buyers.

Many sellers balk when their REALTOR® suggests removing personal items and pieces of furniture that do not show their home to its best advantage. The Stager may bring in new artwork or use slipcovers that are not in keeping with your personal preferences. Remember that you are moving to a new home that you can personalize with your color scheme and furnishings. A more neutral décor is better for the home you are selling.

Now is the time to begin letting go of your home and start looking at it as a house you are selling. Cooperate with your Stager or REALTOR® and let them re-do your rooms. Then, your home photographs and shows in a way that allows your buyers to see themselves living there. They can mentally place their furniture in the rooms and are not distracted by your furnishings. This "love affair" results in offers to purchase.

You need patience and a lot of hard work to get your home ready to show. It takes time to complete all your tasks, pack and remove possessions, and stage your home. But, the pay-off can mean selling your home more quickly and for a higher price.

Promotion

Your REALTOR's® goal is to expose your home to every qualified buyer in the marketplace. More exposure equals a higher sales price and a faster sale. Internet exposure is key to introducing your property to the maximum number of buyers as quickly as possible. With today's technology, your home appears on over 500 real estate websites within 24-48 hours of being entered in your local Multiple Listing Service (MLS).

About 94% of buyers begin their property search on the Internet. And, increasingly, more people access it on their smart phone, iPad or tablet. In December, 2011, buyers spent 94 minutes[4] on their mobile applications (apps) compared to 72 minutes on their desktop computers. Your home needs a powerful presence for both the mobile and desktop audience. Currently, this varies among real estate franchises and independent agencies. When interviewing potential REALTORS®, ask them about their Internet presence and the specific mobile applications they offer. Have them demonstrate these for you.

Pictures create the first impression of your home; their purpose is to help buyers see themselves living there. The quality of your photographs can distinguish your listing from your competition. Both quantity and quality matter. Real estate web sites push listings with the most pictures to the top of

---

[4] John L Scott Real Estate statistics based on usage of their web-based applications.

buyer searches, so you want your REALTOR® to post as many pictures as permitted. He or she may suggest using a professional photographer so your pictures show your home to its best advantage.

You also want maximum neighborhood exposure when your home hits the market. After real estate agents and the Internet, a "For Sale" sign in your yard is your most effective tool for attracting buyers. About 30% of the calls your agent receives come from people who see your sign. Your REALTOR® may attach a flyer box to hold Property Flyers for people who walk or drive by. These flyers include pictures, a description of your home and other information to interest buyers.

In addition, your REALTOR® may send "Just Listed" postcards, and post your listing on their personal blog, website and social media pages. You can help with promoting your home by sending your Listing Flyers to all your friends or posting it to your social media page.

Your REALTOR® probably holds Open Houses where the public may come and look at your home. They also arrange a private showing for agents from their office and the area at large.

The Listing Paperwork

Your next step is to complete all the paperwork for listing your home. Your agent helps you understand each of the forms and gives you a completed copy for your files. You complete a property disclosure statement that describes the current condition of your property. Your REALTOR® writes marketing remarks with a description of your home and directions to it.

The Importance of a Home Warranty

A *Home Warranty* is a home protection plan that provides a service contract to the new owner. It covers the repair or replacement costs for many of the most frequently occurring breakdowns in home appliances and mechanical systems. When a service call is required, the homeowner calls the Home Warranty Company who contacts the appropriate local repair company to make the service call appointment. The homeowner pays a small, set fee that covers time, labor, materials and any follow-up calls related to this repair incident.

The Home Warranty protects the seller from putting money into repairing or replacing appliances or mechanical systems and reduces liability in post-sale issues. The Home Warranty protects your buyer from unexpected repair costs and boosts buyer confidence. You pay the cost of the plan for the first year after the sale closes. Thereafter, your buyer pays for this coverage, if the buyer chooses to continue it.

Showing Your Home

Once your home "goes live" in your Multiple Listing Service, agents call with requests to show it to prospective buyers. Ideally, all an agent has to do is call and leave a message with the time they plan to show your home.

You may have as little as five minutes' notice before the agent and buyer arrive. Sometimes an agent or buyer see the sign in your yard when they're driving to another property, and the buyer says, "Oh, I like that house. Can we take a look at it now?" They may be sitting your driveway when the agent calls! You want agents to have maximum flexibility to show your home at the time the buyer wants to see it. If your home is not available, you may not get a second chance.

If you require an appointment for showing your home, you restrict your buyers and your opportunities to sell. If buyers cannot accommodate your availability, they often move on to other properties. Out-of-town buyers generally cannot wait until a later time.

Buyers feel greater freedom to really look at your home and talk about it with their agent if you are not present. If you're still living in your home, one way you can support the selling process is to be ready to leave on the spur of the moment and take any pets with you. One of my sellers kept a book in the car so he could enjoy reading for as long as his home was being shown. Stay away from your home until you know the agent and buyer are gone.

All-too-often, eager sellers actually cost themselves a sale when they remain and talk with the buyer and their agent. I once listened to a seller talk about a particularly nosy neighbor whom everyone in the neighborhood detested. After we left, I wasn't the least bit surprised when my buyers said they had no interest in living in that neighborhood!

Trust your agent and the buyer's agent to do their jobs. The buyer's agent knows what the buyer is looking for and how to best present your home. If there are questions, the two agents talk, and when necessary, your agent calls you to get answers.

Your REALTOR® places an electronic key box on your front door knob that automatically records the time and name of the agent who shows your home. Your agent contacts all showing agents to get their feedback and shares this information with you.

Every home has a buyer. The goal is to attract this person to view your home and make an offer to purchase it. Your Promotion Plan is designed to sell your home for the highest possible price in the shortest possible time with the least amount of hassle for you.

Receiving an Offer

When your buyer is ready to make an offer, his or her REALTOR® prepares and submits a Residential Real Estate Sale Agreement along with the buyer's earnest money check or promissory note and the lender's Pre-Approval Letter. This letter tells you the buyer is financially qualified to purchase your home. Your REALTOR® carefully reviews the contract with you (and any other people you wish to include in the conversation) so that you understand it completely.

If you do not agree with some parts of the offer, your REALTOR® discusses these with you and prepares a Counter Offer with the terms you want included in the contract and presents this to the buyer's agent. Your agent represents you in negotiations with the buyer until you both agree to all terms and conditions and sign the contract. Remember that the negotiation process almost always requires give and take.

Once the contract is fully accepted, your agent opens Escrow with the title company. The *Escrow Officer* is an independent third party who follows the written instructions from the buyer and the seller for closing the transaction.

The Full House Inspection

Most buyers request a Full House Inspection as one of the conditions of the sale. In Oregon, the buyer pays for the inspection and chooses the inspector. (Laws and practices may differ in other states.) Once the buyer has reviewed the report, he or she may submit a Request for Repairs to the seller. Your REALTOR® explains each item and represents you in negotiations with the buyer until you reach agreement. Repairs should be completed by licensed contractors. The seller pays for these repairs and provides copies of all receipts to show that the work was completed.

The Preliminary Title Report

Your Escrow Officer has several responsibilities. He or she runs a title search and sends you and your buyer the *Preliminary Title Report* showing the condition of the title. It includes the property's legal description, property taxes paid or owing and all liens, if any. This is where your first mortgage and any home equity lines of credit would appear. If there are any other liens such as contractors' liens or spousal support requirements, they would be listed here as well. Your Escrow officer arranges to have all liens paid off. The Escrow Officer gets the exact pay-off amounts from each lienholder and pays them on your behalf from the sale proceeds.

The Loan Approval Process

When your buyers need a loan to purchase your property, they complete their loan application and provide all requested financial information. Once all the paperwork is complete, the loan application is sent to the Underwriter for loan approval.

The lender orders an appraisal of the property. The buyer pays for this. The seller is not entitled to see the appraisal or necessarily know the amount for which the property appraised. If the appraiser notes deficiencies in the condition of the property, the lender may require completion of these repairs before the transaction closes. The seller is responsible for completing these repairs.

Preparing Your Home for Its New Owner

The sales contract states the date on which the seller gives the buyer possession of the property. You need to remove all your personal possessions and complete your final cleaning before that date.

Your buyers appreciate a move-in ready house. Final cleaning includes vacuuming carpets, sweeping floors, cleaning bathrooms and leaving shelving and drawers free of dust and crumbs. Your buyer appreciates receiving all instruction booklets for appliances, the thermostat and other items in the house. Leave these along with extra keys to your home and your garage door openers in a kitchen drawer. As a courtesy, leave toilet paper in each bathroom and paper towels in the kitchen.

Closing the Transaction

The *closing* process places the buyer's name on title as the legal owner and transfers the sales proceeds to the seller. This usually requires 30-45 days, but this period can be much longer, and in some cases, shorter. During this time, required repairs must be completed, any problems from the Title Report must be cleared, the buyer's loan application must be approved, and all conditions of the Sales Contract must be satisfied.

Once final loan approval is received, and all sale conditions are satisfied, the transaction is ready to close. The Escrow officer prepares all the paperwork and sets appointments for both the buyer and seller to come to the office and sign documents. The Escrow officer then sends the buyer's fully signed loan documents back to the Loan Underwriter for final review. When that is completed, the Underwriter issues the notice to Escrow to release funds for closing and recording.

When the Escrow Officer receives approval from the lender to release funds, all paperwork is electronically submitted to the County Assessor's Office where the new owner's name is transferred to title and recorded. Escrow releases the funds to the sellers. Usually the funds are wire-transferred to the account you have specified in your closing instructions to Escrow. Your REALTOR® delivers the keys to your buyer's REALTOR®. The sale transaction is now complete and you are free to pursue the next chapter in your life.

What to Expect When You Move

You are likely to experience an incredibly emotional journey when you move out of your home, especially if you lived in your family home for many years. You are excited about moving to a new home and entering your life's next chapter. But, at the same time, you probably feel deep sadness when you recall the fond memories of the home you are leaving.

After you move into your new home, you need time to feel settled and "at home." Your move is a huge disruption to daily routines and a major transition to new surroundings. Over time, you ease back into old routines or meld them into new ones. This adjustment may take longer than it did when you were younger, so be gentle with yourself and give the process time.

In Conclusion . . .

Where we live matters. This decision is one of the most important choices we make in determining how we meet our changing needs in life's later years. Our homes, neighborhoods, and communities influence whether we have meaningful and satisfying lifestyles.

Like any major lifestyle decision, the key to your success is careful planning for when and where you move. Planning and prevention work. Those who take action to improve the odds of healthy aging and secure their financial future are likely to be successful. But life offers us no guarantees. It takes a little bit of strategy to make sure that you are doing the right thing and that you won't be sorry after the fact.

You move can be rewarding and empowering. We have the prospect of living a long and productive life. It is within our power to make it a celebration.

"For yesterday is already a dream, and tomorrow is only a vision; but today, well lived, makes every yesterday a dream of happiness and every tomorrow a vision of hope. Look well therefore to this day."

From the Sanskrit

Meet Judy Miller

Where you live is an important part of your life. Judy Miller combines her expertise as a REALTOR® and CERTIFIED FINANCIAL PLANNER™ professional in introducing Residence Planning, a process to guide people in defining what they need in their homes during the second half of life. Her goals include helping people determine the best time to move while protecting the value of their home.

Miller's background uniquely qualifies her for her role in Residence Planning. She spent 20 years in business, including serving as an Assistant Vice President with Citicorp in Manhattan and California before opening her own practice in financial planning. She holds many professional designations in real estate and financial planning. Her Master's degree in Education has contributed to her passion to educate and coach individuals on wise life choices.

She is active in professional and community organizations and serves as an Elder in her church. In her free time, she enjoys her three grandchildren and romping on the beach with her dog.

Miller holds the following designations:

The **CERTIFIED FINANCIAL PLANNER™** professional designation is granted to those who complete the extensive education requirements in insurance, tax, estate and investments, and meet the CFP Board's ethics, experience, and examination requirements.

The Certified Residential Specialist®, a designation held by only 3% of all REALTORS®, is awarded to those who have completed specialized education in residential sales and demonstrated proven sales performance.

Certified Senior Advisors® use their broad-based knowledge of health, social and financial issues and the dynamics of how these factors work together in seniors' lives to build and increase understanding for quality of living and financial security.

Graduate REALTOR® Institute (GRI®), a designation held by only 19% of REALTORS®, covers contracts, professional standards, sales, marketing, finance and risk reduction.

Seniors Real Estate Specialist (SRES®) designees receive education on tax laws, probate, estate planning, equity conversion strategies, reverse mortgages, the uses of pensions, 401k accounts, and IRAs in real estate transactions.

Self-Assessment: Are You Living in the Right House?

Complete the following Self-Assessment to get a sense of whether your lifestyle needs suggest you move to a different home. This is not a test with right or wrong answers. The goal is to give you a clearer picture so you are in a position to make well-informed choices as you move forward.

Have your spouse, sibling, adult child or very close friend complete it based on their knowledge of you. You may gain valuable insights by comparing answers. If their answers differ from yours, talk about the differences. Your goal is to be as objective and honest about yourself as possible.

You may come back in several years and complete it again. Then compare responses at that time with your original responses.

The goal is to make good decisions for your future. The points merely provide guidance in making well-informed choices.

Self-Assessment: Are You Living in the Right House?

One of the ways to determine the answer to this question is by candidly answering a few questions. Respond to the following statements by circling your answer using this scale:

1 = Strongly Disagree 2 = Disagree 3 = Neutral
4 = Agree   5 = Strongly Agree

1	2	3	4	5	I am financially sound.
1	2	3	4	5	I have a "Rainy Day Fund" sufficient to cover living expenses for four-six months. I can maintain this fund on an ongoing basis.
1	2	3	4	5	I can afford the property taxes and insurance premiums for my home.
1	2	3	4	5	I can financially support my home expenses so that I can enjoy living there over the long term.
					TOTAL for Page 1

1	2	3	4	5	I am physically able to maintain my home (cleaning, laundry, changing beds, vacuuming) the way I want it. I don't have to hire help or ask others to help.
1	2	3	4	5	I **ENJOY** maintaining my home (cleaning, laundry, changing beds, vacuuming) the way I want it.
1	2	3	4	5	I am physically able to maintain my yard and landscaping the way I want it.
1	2	3	4	5	I **ENJOY** maintaining my yard and landscaping the way I want it.
1	2	3	4	5	I can find good workers (handyman, plumber, electrician, yard person, house cleaner, etc.) to take care of my home.
					TOTAL for Page 2

1	2	3	4	5	I can financially afford to replace the mechanical systems (heating/air conditioning, plumbing, roof, water, kitchen appliances, etc.) in my home when required.
1	2	3	4	5	I am able to get to my doctors and medical facilities easily for appointments and tests.
1	2	3	4	5	I am comfortable handling an emergency in my home (accident, major health emergency, fire, police).
1	2	3	4	5	I feel safe and secure in my home and neighborhood. I don't worry about people breaking into my home.

TOTAL for Page 3

1	2	3	4	5	My family believes I am safe and secure in my home and they are fully supportive of my living here.
1	2	3	4	5	I pay my bills on time, balance my checkbook, track my credit card charges and file my insurance claims regularly.
1	2	3	4	5	I get about easily to run errands and go places. I am comfortable that I am a safe driver, both day and night.
1	2	3	4	5	I don't worry about being a burden to my family or friends.
1	2	3	4	5	I would be able to manage in my home if I had physical limitations (sight, hearing, mobility and stairs).

TOTAL for Page 4

1	2	3	4	5	My home is set up to handle these changes.
1	2	3	4	5	I communicate comfortably with my family about my lifestyle needs. I am not experiencing emotional conflict from them.
1	2	3	4	5	I am not concerned about health changes or restrictions limiting my ability to live in my home.
1	2	3	4	5	I bring in my groceries to the kitchen. I prepare and eat nutritious meals regularly.
1	2	3	4	5	I have thought about how I can continue to live here if my ability to manage my home declines. My home can accommodate these changes.
					TOTAL for Page 5

1 2 3 4 5 | I am socially involved with my friends, clubs and groups I belong to. I visit with people outside my home at least once a week.

1 2 3 4 5 | Maintaining my independence in my own home is very important to me.

[ ] | **TOTAL for Page 6**

After you have answered all the questions, transfer your totals for each page to the rows below.

[ ] | **TOTAL for Page 1**

[ ] | **TOTAL for Page 2**

[ ] | **TOTAL for Page 3**

[ ] | **TOTAL for Page 4**

[ ] | **TOTAL for Page 5**

[ ] | **TOTAL for Page 6**

[ ] | **GRAND TOTAL**

Guide to Understanding Your Total Points

54 points or below   Suggests you immediately look at alternatives to your current situation and make changes soon.

55 to 95 points   Suggests you begin exploring options for moving to a Residence Community or other supervised living arrangement. The time is approaching when this is a good decision for you to make.

96 and above   Suggests you may take your time choosing how, when and where you move later in your retirement years.

If you want quality living in a home that maximizes your investment, you want to work with Judy Miller.

Judy offers a complimentary one-hour consultation to help you explore options and get answers to your questions. She is happy to provide a *Market Value Report* for your home and a copy of this book. Call today and schedule your appointment.

Judy Miller, Broker
541.941.6201
Toll Free: 800.888.5706
Email: judymiller@johnlscott.com
www.JudyMillerRealEstate.com

871 Medford Center
Medford, OR 97504

Made in the USA
Charleston, SC
22 June 2013